CW01511355

Your dinner's in the dog

Your dinner's in the dog

Peter Coupe

INDEX

Published by Arcturus Publishing Limited
For Index,
Unit 1
Garrard Way
Kettering
NN16 8TD

This edition published 1996

All rights reserved. No part of this publication may be reproduced, stored in a
retrieval system, or transmitted, in any form or by any means, electronic,
mechanical, photocopying, recording, or otherwise, without written
permission or in accordance with the provisions of the Copyright Act 1956
(as amended). Any person or persons who do any unauthorised act in
relation to this publication may be liable to criminal prosecution and civil
claims for damages.

Printed and bound in Great Britain

© Arcturus Publishing Limited
443 Oxford Street
London W1R 1DA

ISBN 1 900032 51 1

If you have a "New Man" in your life, but are still having to do all the ironing, shopping and toilet cleaning, this book is for you.

Woman are people after all; and can be as crafty, sly and downright dishonest as men – when it suits them.

This book is definately not a guide to the perfect relationship; but rest assured that it doesn't contain any recipes or fashion tips either.

In this witty and acerbic collection of cartoons we can see how women finish up on top far more often than the men in their lives would have us believe.

JUST A SMALL BOTTLE — ENOUGH TO SHIFT THE BALANCE OF POWER DURING WIMBLEDON FORTNIGHT!

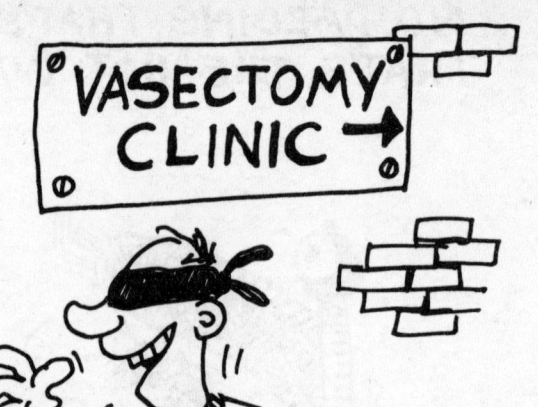

WELL — I'LL CERTAINLY NEVER DOUBT THE POWER OF WITCHCRAFT AGAIN...

YOUR "BLIND DATE" SAW YOU THROUGH THE WINDOW — AND SHE'LL SEE YOU AND THE DATING AGENCY IN COURT!

ISN'T HE LOVELY — AND JUST LIKE HIS FATHER —
EVEN THE BIRTHMARK ON HIS
BOTTOM IS THE SAME...

WE MAKE LOVE WHENEVER ENGLAND WIN
A MATCH — I HAVE SOME LOVELY MEMORIES
OF 1966...

MR. WILSON - YOUR WIFE JUST CALLED - SHE'S
FOUND OUT ABOUT OUR AFFAIR AND WANTS
TO KNOW IF YOU WANT YOUR CLOTHES
SHREDDED OR BURNED...

YES, MARTIN, WOMEN DO LIKE MEN WHO CAN
MAKE THEM LAUGH...
        ... BUT THERE'S A TIME AND
        PLACE FOR IT!..

THE SPARKLE HAS GONE OUT OF OUR RELATIONSHIP - HE ONLY EVER WANTS TO MAKE LOVE IN THE BEDROOM THESE DAYS...

IT'S EASY TO TELL YOU WERE AN ONLY CHILD ~
YOU NEVER LEARNED TO COME SECOND...

– AND AFTER THE BREAK WE'LL BE LOOKING AT A SILLY REPORT WHICH CLAIMS THAT SOME T.V. PRESENTERS GET THE JOB THROUGH SEX APPEAL RATHER THAN JOURNALISTIC ABILITY...

WE'VE BEEN SAVING FOR FIVE YEARS FOR AN EXTENSION – AND THIS IS WHERE WE'RE GOING TO GET IT!

IT'S ABOUT TIME YOU MADE
SOMETHING OF YOURSELF!

OH! I **LOVE** HONEYMOONS, DON'T YOU?

WELL - YOU SAID YOU WANTED TO GO SOMEWHERE
YOU'VE NEVER BEEN BEFORE...

SHE'S JUST HAD MAJOR PLASTIC SURGERY — THE BANK CONFISCATED ALL HER CREDIT CARDS!

CAN'T TALK NOW — MARTIN WANTS TO MAKE LOVE — CALL YOU BACK IN TWO MINUTES!

— DON'T THEY NORMALLY PUT SECURITY VIDEO CAMERAS ON THE CEILING?!

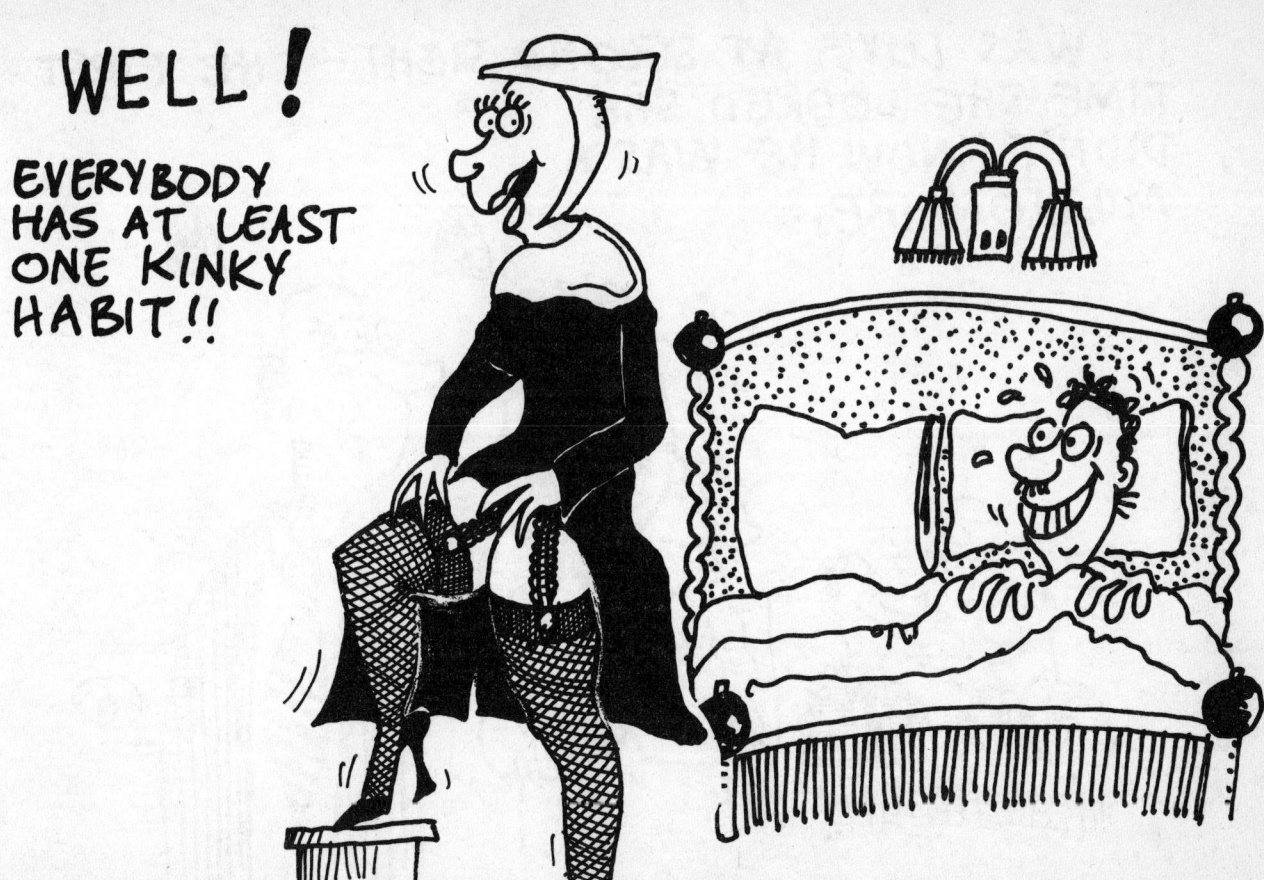

IT WAS LOVE AT SECOND SIGHT – THE FIRST TIME SHE LOOKED SHE DIDN'T KNOW HE WAS A MILLIONAIRE...

MY BOYFRIEND USED TO KISS ME ON THE LIPS-
BUT IT'S ALL OVER NOW!

IF YOU GO BALD AT THE FRONT IT MEANS YOU'RE SEXY -
IF YOU GO BALD AT THE BACK IT MEANS YOU'RE A THINKER -

YOU OBVIOUSLY THINK A LOT ABOUT SEX !

OF COURSE I TALK TO MY HUSBAND WHEN I'M MAKING LOVE – IF HE TELEPHONES...

MY HUSBAND IS GREAT IN BED — HE SHOULD BE,
HE CERTAINLY GETS ENOUGH PRACTISE...

—HELLO, DARLING, YOU'RE HOME EARLY. COME INSIDE' AND I'LL TELL YOU ALL ABOUT MY NEW JOB...

...NO GOOD HIDING — IT'S FRIDAY NIGHT!

-HELLO, MISS. BROWN,
JUST RINGING TO CONFIRM
THAT THE MEASUREMENT
I GAVE YOU SHOULD BE
IN INCHES...
... NOT CENTIMETRES!